巴拉克·奥巴马

Heroes and Role Models | Non-Fiction Series

Copyright © 2022 by Level Learning, INC. and Washington Yu Ying PCS™
Original and Edited Text Copyright © 2022 by Washington Yu Ying PCS™

All rights reserved. No part of this book in whole or part may be reproduced without written permission from the publisher.

Published by Level Learning, INC.
Content Contributors:
Washington Yu Ying PCS™ - Teng Shen, Pearl Zao He You
Level Learning - Jingyao Qi

Illustrations by: Matt Austin

Leveling classification based on Level Learning standard.
For full description, visit www.levellearning.com

ISBN 978-1-64040-017-7
Simplified Chinese Edition

About Level Learning:
Level Learning provides a literacy focused curriculum specifically designed for K-12 Chinese as a Second Language classrooms. Our program offers 20 levels of specific and detailed objectives, leveled texts and passages, mastery-based online assessment, and analytics to enable data-driven instruction. Level Learning reading curriculum for both literature and informational text emphasize grammar and comprehension skills to help teachers develop confident and independent Chinese language readers. The non-fiction series of books are specifically designed to support our informational text course based on multiple national standards. To learn more about our entire offering, visit www.levellearning.com.

About Washington Yu Ying PCS™:
Washington Yu Ying PCS is a Mandarin English dual language immersion International Baccalaureate (IB) World school. Yu Ying's mission is to inspire and prepare young people to create a better world by challenging them to reach their full potential in a nurturing Chinese/English educational environment. Yu Ying's comprehensive IB, dual immersion curriculum equips students with global competencies for success in the real world. As a leader in immersion education, Yu Ying is determined to advance Chinese language programs and global citizenry education by helping other schools create and strengthen their Chinese programs. For more information, email: products@washingtonyuying.org

巴拉克·奥巴马是美国第44任总统。他也是美国第一任非洲裔总统。

1961年，奥巴马出生在美国的夏威夷州。小时候的奥巴马因为自己的肤色，经常受到不公平的对待，这让他很难过。

奥巴马从纽约市哥伦比亚大学毕业以后,来到芝加哥工作。那时候,他帮助了很多当地的穷人。为了帮助更多的人,他想要成为一名律师。所以,他又去了哈佛大学法律系学习。

奥巴马从哈佛大学毕业后,又回到了芝加哥工作。1996年,奥巴马被选为伊利诺伊州参议员。2004年,他成为美国参议院的参议员。

2008年,奥巴马成为美国总统。在他的努力下,美国和伊拉克的战争结束了。2009年,他得到了"诺贝尔和平奖"。

奥巴马关心人民的平等权利。在他当总统时，他提高最低收入，减少税收，他还提出了新的医疗法案。他的很多做法都受到美国人民的欢迎。

2017年1月，奥巴马八年的总统工作结束了。在他的告别演讲里，他鼓励人们继续为自由和平等而努力。

Glossary

	Pinyin	English Definition
总统	zǒng tǒng	president
非洲裔	fēi zhōu yì	African descent
夏威夷州	xià wēi yí zhōu	State of Hawaii
肤色	fū sè	skin color
公平	gōng píng	equally
对待	duì dài	treatment
难过	nán guò	sad
纽约市	niǔ yuē shì	New York City
哥伦比亚大学	gē lún bǐ yà dà xué	Columbia University
毕业	bì yè	to graduate
芝加哥	zhī jiā gē	Chicago
律师	lǜ shī	lawyer
哈佛大学	hā fó dà xué	Harvard University
法律系	fǎ lǜ xì	law school

	Pinyin	English Definition
利诺伊州	yī lì nuò yī zhōu	Illinois
议员	cān yì yuán	senator
国参议院	měi guó cān yì yuàn	Unites States Senate
拉克	yī lā kè	Iraq
争	zhàn zhēng	war
束	jié shù	end
贝尔和平	nuò bèi ěr hé píng jiǎng	Nobel Peace Prize
等权利	píng děng quán lì	equal rights
低收入	zuì dī shōu rù	minimum wage
收	shuì shōu	tax
出	tí chū	to propose
疗	yī liáo	medical care
案	fǎ àn	law

	Pinyin	English Definition
受到	shòu dào	to receive
告别	gào bié	farewell
演讲	yǎn jiǎng	speech
鼓励	gù lì	to encourage
自由	zì yóu	freedom

www.ingramcontent.com/pod-product-compliance
Lightning Source LLC
Chambersburg PA
CBHW041224070526
44584CB00001B/88